Life With God

LOVE IN ACTION

Helen Johns

Evangel Publishing House

Nappanee, Indiana 46550

Cover photograph: FotoSearch Stock Photography
Cover design: Matthew Gable
Library of Congress Catalog Card Number: 89-84627
ISBN-10: 0-916035-28-X
ISBN-13: 978-0-916035-28-0

Spanish edition also available:
La Vida con Dios: Amor en Acción
ISBN-10: 0-916035-45-X
ISBN-13: 978-0-916035-45-7

PHOTOTYPESET FOR QUALITY

Printed in the United States of America

10 9 8 7 6 5 4 3

Contents

Introduction

In 1900, a hymn writer penned this prayer, "Deeper, deeper in the love of Jesus daily let me go; higher, higher in the school of wisdom, more of grace to know." Like the plant pictured on the cover of the second book in this *Life With God* series, you have put down roots in your Christian life that are growing deeper and more firmly planted in God's wisdom and love. In *Basics for New Christians*, you began the disciplines of prayer, Bible study, fellowship, and worship. You received first instructions in overcoming fear, doubts, and temptations, and in telling others of your faith.

This study, *Love in Action*, will help you continue to sink roots into the rich soil of Bible study and fellowship as you work through the topics with your friends or small group. As you experience the sunshine of God's daily presence, you will grow up and out toward other persons. God will begin to express Christ's love through you. By tapping into love's power source—the Holy Spirit—you will begin to build a life of service and giving, and of peaceful, restored relationships. By committing yourself to a pure and holy life, you will continue to grow into a lasting relationship with Christ the Lord.

As you did in *Basics for New Christians*, read the short chapters, do the "Check It Out" questions, and discuss the "Talk It Over" sections. A new feature in this book is the "Up Close and Personal" sections which encourage you to study longer passages of Scripture. You will also find Bible passages to memorize, Bible reading plans, and a prayer journal at the end of the book.

As you study, perhaps your prayer will become that of the song writer: "Deeper, deeper . . . rooted in the holy love of Jesus, let me fruitful grow."*

*Charles P. Jones, "Deeper, Deeper," page 450 in *Hymns for Praise and Worship*, © 1984, Evangel Press, Nappanee, IN 46550.

1

Love in Action

Consider this statement: If all God wants is a loving relationship with you, he would have taken you to heaven at the moment you believed in Jesus Christ as your Savior. What do you think? Why does God leave us in the world? Could it be that he has a purpose for each of us? If so, what is it?

These are not easy questions. But many of the answers lie in understanding the central character in the history of mankind— Jesus Christ. You already know some facts about Jesus. Let's see what one Scripture has to say about this extraordinary person:

*He is the image of the invisible God, the firstborn over all creation. For by him all things were created: things in heaven and on earth, visible and invisible, whether thrones or powers or rulers or authorities; all things were created by him and for him. And he is the head of the body, the church; he is the beginning and the firstborn from among the dead, so that in everything he might have the supremacy—*Colossians 1:15-18.

You may have known that Christ came to earth as a man, that he came without possessions or power, that he died a humiliating death and rose again so we also can have eternal life. But did you realize that he now is the supreme ruler, the head of everything that exists? He is the beginning and the end of everything. His authority has no limits.

Accepting Jesus' authority

Christians and non-Christians alike generally have little difficulty understanding Christ the teacher, the man. But even Christians have trouble grasping the scope of Christ's authority. Jesus himself said, "All authority in heaven and on earth has been given to me" (Matthew 28:18). Even the disciples, the closest friends of Jesus, had an incomplete understanding of who he was. When Jesus performed a miracle, they exclaimed, "Who is this? Even the wind and the waves obey him!" (Mark 4:41). It is almost amusing to think that Satan, trying to tempt Jesus after his baptism, offered Jesus authority over all the kingdoms of the earth if Jesus would bow down and worship him (Matthew 4:8-9). The irony is, ultimate power already belonged to Jesus.

If you are one of those people who have trouble with the concept of Jesus as "Lord," don't be alarmed. Many people, especially North Americans, do not respond well to such words as lord, king, authority, obedience, and submission. A mistaken concept of freedom leads us to believe that we are our own master in every situation. And we sometimes guard that so-called freedom—the power of self-determination, and the power to pursue happiness at any cost—to the point of harming ourselves and other people.

Also, we have not learned to fully trust God. We think, "God may ask me to do something I don't want to do." Or, "God will take away all my pleasures." Or, "I know what is best for me. How can God possibly know better?" Or, "Maybe God doesn't really have my best interests in mind."

Moreover, many of us are seemingly very capable of managing our own lives. Before we were Christians, life actually may have been easier in the respect that we made decisions based on our own self-interest. We didn't know we could and should seek God's opinion, so we didn't make the effort. The results of our choices may have turned out looking all right to the world, but they may not have been what God wanted.

*At the name of Jesus every knee
should bow . . . and every tongue
confess that Jesus Christ is Lord.*

Philippians 2:10-11

Beyond salvation

When you became a Christian, you confessed your sin and took Christ as your Savior. Entrance into the family of God was a decisive, one-time act that set in motion all kinds of good consequences. But because of the lingering effects of our "old" nature, even Christians still tend to be self-willed people. The act of placing Christ and his authority at the center of our thoughts and actions—replacing our own selfishness with God's will—must be an intentional act, followed by daily recommitment. Jesus said, "If anyone would come after me, he must deny himself and take up his cross *daily* and follow me" (Luke 9:23).

Each day brings new decisions, new temptations, new opportunities. Think for a moment about all of the different areas of your life and the decisions they entail. Some of the major areas are career, life partner, children, money and possessions, education, leisure time, friends, where you live, and daily plans. It is easy to get side-tracked and fail to ask for, learn about, or follow God's guidance. When we don't focus our attention on Jesus, when we don't give him our first and our best, we tend to wander out of the reach of his instruction onto paths that lead away from God and his best for us. Jesus came so we could "have life and have it to the full" (John 10:10). But the fulfillment of that promise comes in direct proportion to how many of our daily choices we turn over to God.

God deserves our trust

All of this sounds rather scary unless we understand God's character and motivation. We normally don't like to feel that life is "out of our control." In the world, people may strive and even fight for freedom against their rulers. Even in a democracy, we are accustomed to finding fault with and resisting those in government. But in God's kingdom, we are privileged to follow God's rule because we trust it will result in the best for us and others, even if we don't totally understand how or why. No doubt, God will ask us to do some things we don't want to do or think we can't do. And yes, he asks us to serve him at some cost to our worldly comfort. But God *is* love, and he knows the future; we don't. It is far wiser to follow God, who can see the end of the path. We can only see a few feet ahead.

The story of Jesus is the account of God's active love, in which God proved by positive action that he deserves our trust. In 1 John 3:16, love is defined in terms of action: "This is how we know what love is: Jesus Christ *laid down* his life for us. Romans 5:8 says, "God *demonstrates* his own love for us in this: while we were still sinners, Christ *died* for us." One of the most often quoted passages is John 3:16: "God so loved the world that he *gave* his one and only Son, that whosoever believes in him shall not perish but have eternal life." God loves you so much that he took action. He sent Jesus—his beloved, perfect, only Son—to die in your place. God was active in the world then, and still is today. He cares for you and desires to guide you through each day.

Our response

The Bible is also quite clear that we are to respond by becoming God's servants. "Do you not know," asks Paul in 1 Corinthians 6:19-20, "that your body is a temple of the Holy Spirit, who is in you, whom you have received from God? You are not your own; you were bought with a price." The price was the suffering and shed blood of Jesus. So, we either serve sin— our own misguided, selfish desires—or we serve Jesus. Our choice is to remain in a life of inactivity or wrong-doing, or to voluntarily enlist in Christ's service.

Whether we choose Christ's authority or not, he is still in control. A full, abundant, joyful Christian life is a matter of acknowledging that control and aligning ourselves with God's purposes. We allow God's way to prevail when we can say, "Lord, please tell me what you want me to do and be. Help me break the habit of doing only what I want, and give me the wisdom and strength to follow you."

When we walk with Jesus, desiring to do what he wants and accepting his authority—whether it is made clear to us through prayer, Bible study, or the counsel of other believers in the church—God can put his love into action through us. The Holy Spirit lives within us to help us respond to God's active love with active service. To answer one of the questions that began this chapter, we are here to serve and glorify God. We are not to sit back, content only to be saved from our past sin. God now has an action-filled, dynamic plan for us all. Finding elements of that plan is what this book will help us begin to do.

When you prayed the prayer of repentance to receive salvation, you may have said something like, "I open the door of my life and receive Jesus as my Savior . . ." In the same breath, you probably said, ". . . and Lord." Perhaps now, having studied the Bible and talked with other Christians, you are searching for a deeper, fuller understanding of the meaning of Jesus as "Lord" in your heart and life. If so, talk it over with your pastor or Christian friend. You are well on your way to becoming all that God wants you to be!

☑ Check It Out

These Bible questions and answers are drawn from the New International Version. You may use other versions, but your answers may vary. Answers begin on p. 62.

1. Who do these verses say that Jesus is?

   (a) John 13:13 _____

   (b) Acts 2:36 _____

   (c) Revelation 19:16 _____

   (d) Romans 14:9 _____

2. According to 2 Corinthians 5:15, why did Jesus die? _____

   _____

   _____

3. Where is Jesus now (Hebrews 1:1-4)? (a) _____

   _____

   How shall he be treated (Philippians 2:9-11)? (b) _____

   _____

4. List the three instructions in Proverbs 3:5-6 and the results.

   (a) _____

   (b) _____

   (c) _____

   (d) results: _____

5. According to Proverbs 3:11-12, we should not despise the Lord's _____ , because he loves us.

6. What are the promises in Psalm 32:8? _____

_____

_____

7. What do you think Jesus means in Matthew 11:28-30 when he says, "Take my yoke upon you and learn from me"? _____

_____

_____

8. What does John urge us to do in 1 John 3:18? _____

_____

9. Read James 2:14-26. According to James in verse 22, (a) _____ and (b) _____ work together.

10. Loving God means _____ his commands (1 John 5:3).

Talk It Over

1. Take a few moments to assess your personal relationship with God. Evaluate your growth in each of these areas: Bible study, prayer, fellowship with the Church, confronting temptation and fears, and witnessing. How do you think these personal disciplines are related to the Lordship of Jesus in your life?

2. Talk about how your ideas about freedom may have changed after reading about Christ as Lord. In what way is allowing Christ to rule our lives a liberating idea?

3. What specific situations or habits in your life are difficult to give to the Lord? Can you pinpoint the reasons that it is hard to allow the Lord to fully rule in these situations?

4. Say out loud a one- or two-sentence prayer thanking God for sending Jesus, telling God what that action has meant personally to you. Then ask God to fill you with his love and help you find ways this week to put that love into action through you.

 # Up Close and Personal

Meet Paul. Read Acts 6:8-10; Acts 7:54—8:2; Acts 9:1-22; and Acts 26:1-20 (Paul's own account of his conversion).

1. What kind of person was Paul (called Saul) before his conversion?

2. What immediate and long-term effects did meeting Jesus on the road to Damascus have on Paul?

3. What impact could (or did) recognizing Jesus as Lord have on you?

Tips on Christian decision-making

When attempting to discover *God's will,* we need to realize that the term can have different meanings:

A. God's *sovereign* will—God's hidden plan that oversees everything that happens in the universe.

B. God's *moral* will—God's revealed commands in the Bible that teach people how to believe and live.

C. God's *individual* will—God's ideal, detailed life-plan uniquely designed for each person.[1]

Some decisions don't fall under any of the above. For example, God probably approves of either the green or the blue hand towel in the bathroom cabinet. Don't get tied in knots over little things. But learn to be spiritually sensitive to which decisions are important in God's plan for you.

Many decisions will entail finding out whether the situation falls under "B" or "C" above. In cases governed by "B"—God's revealed will—test your decision on these grounds:

1. Does it agree with Scripture? If not, there is no longer any decision to make. God has made it for you.

2. Is it right? Does it align with God's character as revealed in Jesus Christ?[2]

continued on next page

If the situation falls under category "C"—God's individual will—*also* test your decision on these grounds:

1. What direction is the Holy Spirit giving in prayer?

2. What advice are you hearing from people in the church? Are you aligning yourself with the beliefs of your local church family? (Go and *seek* their counsel.)

3. Is it reasonable? Ponder John Wesley's warning: "Do not hastily ascribe things to God. Do not easily suppose dreams, voices, impressions, visions, or revelations to be from God. They may be from him. They may be nature. They may be from the devil. Therefore, believe not every spirit, but 'try the spirits whether they be from God.' "

4. Watch for confirming circumstances—"open doors." Give God all the time you can to move in the situation, but don't necessarily sit around and wait for a miraculous sign.

5. Obey, then trust. Scripture says God's individual guidance is like a lamp for our feet, not necessarily a beacon miles ahead. God rarely defines our future course so clearly that action requires no faith.

6. Realize decisions which seem to turn out wrong do not end your relationship with God. Ask for forgiveness if necessary, and go on, confident that God still loves you.

---

[1]*Decision Making and the Will of God,* Garry Friesen with J. Robin Maxson, © 1980, Multnomah Press, Portland, Oregon 97266.

[2]*Impressions,* Martin Wells Knapp, first published, 1892, © 1984 by God's Bible School, Cincinnati, Ohio, printed by Tyndale Press.

2

Love's Power Source

Close your eyes for a moment and imagine a soft, warm breeze blowing against your face. Or take some time to remember pictures or actual experiences of a tornado or hurricane. Or imagine yourself standing barefoot next to a door in the wintertime, feeling the exhilaration of the outside air swirling past your toes. What causes these feelings and effects is not something you can hold or see. But the wind, the moving air, is nonetheless quite real. So it is with the Holy Spirit. Though we cannot touch him, we know this person is real and active.

Jesus was the living picture of God that people could see. Limited in his earthly existence to one place and time, he told his followers that it was necessary for him to go away. Someone else was to come—God in a different form—who could be everywhere at once and enter as the life-giving breath of God into every Christian. This Holy Spirit now lives in us to give us the power to accomplish God's purposes.

Love's cleansing
Even before you came to Christ, the Holy Spirit was working in your life, giving you a sense of your own sin, helping you to know what is right, and then influencing you until you finally stopped resisting God. You can be thankful that God the Spirit

took this active interest in you as a special individual, and worked in you until you were born into a new life.

Now that you are a Christian, you can have the full benefits of the Holy Spirit's presence. When Christians give full control of ourselves to God, we are "filled up" as if we had a river flowing from deep within. We are saturated with love which is then able to overflow into our actions and relationships.

One purpose of the Holy Spirit is to penetrate the dirty, dark places in our lives and to clean them up. It may be helpful to think of this in terms of the rooms of a house. Some of us invite the Holy Spirit to clean the living and dining rooms and kitchen—the public, visible places—but never open the door and let him into the basement, closet, bath, or bedroom. The Spirit desires to change us through and through, perfecting us totally.

After our initial commitment to Christ, this becomes an everyday process. The Holy Spirit is in us to help in every aspect of life. When we sin, the Spirit troubles our conscience, leading us to confession and forgiveness. When we hurt, he comforts. When we are confused or need guidance, we may ask for and receive teaching and wisdom. The Holy Spirit speaks to us through our "inner ear," giving us knowledge of the mysteries of life through teaching, Scripture, and prayer. He gives us strength when we face temptation and deal with our own weaknesses. He leads us away from sin. And when we can't pray, the Spirit offers prayers to God for us, and gives renewed life, hope, and peace.

Power to serve

The Holy Spirit calls us to follow God's plan for our lives instead of our own, and gives us directions for action. What's more, after we receive our instructions, the Spirit does not leave us alone to try to attain those goals. If we would look up the hundreds of references to the Spirit in the Bible, we often would find a mention of power close by. For example, we read in Ephesians 3:16-20 that God can accomplish through us "more than all we ask or imagine, according to his *power* that is at work within us." All that is required of us is an openness to the Holy

*The one who sows to please the
Spirit, from the Spirit will
reap eternal life.*

Galatians 6:8b

Spirit coupled with faith and a growing realization of how strong and wonderful our God really is.

God wants to work *in* us, making us more and more like Christ. Little by little, through the experiences of life and the teachings of the Bible and other Christians, we learn what the qualities are (sometimes called "fruit") that God wants to see in us. Many of them are listed in various portions of Scripture (see Question 2, Check It Out, p. 20). In John, chapter 15, Jesus helps us understand how we go about growing in these areas when he says: "I am the vine, you are the branches. If a man remains in me and I in him, he will bear much fruit. . . . Now remain in my love." We remain "connected" to Christ and are able to change our attitudes and actions through the ministry of the Holy Spirit.

God also wants to work *through* us to build his kingdom. To accomplish this, God gives special abilities, or "gifts" of the Spirit, enabling us to do things far beyond our natural capabilities. These gifts are not for selfish use, but rather are meant to further God's purposes within the church. We are instructed to eagerly desire and use spiritual gifts, always remembering that whatever we do is to be done in love, with the good of others in mind. (See *Life With God: Basics for New Christians*, Chapter 4, pp. 28, 31 for more on the gifts of the Spirit.)

Power in the church

By now, perhaps you are beginning to see why you are so different from your non-Christian friends or family members. It is this presence of God the Spirit who lives in you which makes you different in every significant way. John 14:17 says that "the world cannot accept him, because it neither sees him nor knows him. But you know him, for he [the Spirit] lives with you and . . . in you."

Not only does the Holy Spirit reside within you as an individual, but the presence of the Holy Spirit is what makes the church unique. When we gather together as the local congregation, God manifests himself in wonderful ways to be found in no other organization. The Holy Spirit enables the church to live and work together in unity. Because of this oneness of love and purpose, the church can become a collective witness of the power of Christ. One song explains, "they will know we are Christians by our love." These words speak of the way God can accomplish more on earth through us *together* than is possible if we were individual Christians, functioning alone.

So, we can see that the Holy Spirit is God's great gift to us as individuals and to the church. As a pre-payment of the joys of heaven, the Holy Spirit brings us assurance and peace. Using the strength of our diversity as individuals within the church to mold us into the body of Christ on earth, the Spirit delights in sharing with us the resources and power of God. We need to recognize and use the Spirit's power. God wants us to have a life of overflowing power, ability, and love.

☑ Check It Out

1. Match the qualities and functions of the Holy Spirit on the left
   with each Scripture on the right.

A. Convicter of the world's sin   _____ Acts 1:8

B. testifies about Jesus   _____ Acts 4:31

C. enables us to speak the   _____ Acts 9:31
   Word of God boldly   _____ 1 Corinthians 3:16

D. gives us a mind filled with   _____ Ephesians 4:3
   life and peace   _____ Ephesians 1:13-14

E. is a deposit guaranteeing   _____ John 14:26
   our inheritance from God   _____ John 15:26-27

F. Counselor, teacher   _____ John 16:8-11

G. gives power to witness   _____ Romans 5:5

H. is more powerful than the   _____ Romans 8:6
   evil one   _____ Romans 15:17-19

I. lives within Christians   _____ 1 John 4:4

J. fills our hearts with love

K. strengthens and encourages

L. accomplishes signs and
   miracles so that the gospel
   might be proclaimed

M. gives Christians unity
   through the bond of peace

2. Read Galatians 5:22-23, Colossians 3:12-14, and 2 Peter 1:5-7. When the Holy Spirit controls our lives, he produces in us:

_____

_____

_____

_____

_____

 ## Talk It Over

1. Go back over the list of attributes, jobs, and effects of the Holy Spirit in Questions 1 and 2 of Check It Out. Are there any passages you didn't understand? Talk about the times since you have been a Christian when you noticed the Holy Spirit was at work in your life. When have you seen the Spirit working for or in other Christians?

2. Is it difficult for you to accept the fact that God lives within you? Why or why not? What difference does it make to you in (a) the care of your body, (b) your understanding of eternal life, (c) your acceptance of your responsibility to try to witness, love others, and do the right things?

3. What "rooms" of your life do you still need to open to the Spirit to "clean up"? Do you have sin which needs to be confessed or a habit which you need the Holy Spirit's power to overcome? If so, take time to (a) *admit* the need, (b) *ask* for God's forgiveness, (c) *ask* for God's help, (d) *give* the situation totally into God's care, and (e) confidently *receive* the Spirit's power to conquer the problem.

4. If you have not previously done so in another study, review the gifts of the Spirit listed in 1 Corinthians 12:8-10 and Romans 12:6-8. Have your discussion leader or friend share with you some evidences of this special gifting from God he or she may have observed or experienced.

 # Up Close and Personal

Peter at Pentecost. Read Acts 1:1-8; and Acts 2:1-41. (Pentecost was the name of a feast day when Jews gathered in Jerusalem from near and far.)

1. The Holy Spirit's coming was to bring power so the disciples could become what? What was the immediate result of the Holy Spirit's coming? (2:41)

2. What do you know or can you find out about the kind of person Peter was before Pentecost? (See Matthew 4:18-20; 16:13-18; 26:57-75.) Do you suppose Peter could have taken leadership and preached the "first sermon" (verses 14-36) without the Holy Spirit?

3. How has the Holy Spirit changed your life?

Tips on keeping your balance

As Christians, we acknowledge that the Holy Spirit is vitally important to us, and we are thankful for this presence of God in and among us. So it is not surprising that some Christians seem to overemphasize the Holy Spirit, while others limit his ministry to the point of contradicting the truth of Scripture. In John 16:14-15, Jesus makes a strong claim of authority, something he knew Christians might tend to forget: "When the Spirit of truth comes, he will guide you into all truth. He will not speak on his own; he will speak only what he hears, and he will tell you what is yet to come. He will bring glory to me. . . ." Another time, Jesus said, "The Counselor, the Holy Spirit, whom the Father sent *in my name*, will teach you all things and will remind you of everything I have said to you" (John 14:26).

Do you see where Christ focused the authority? Squarely on himself. It is not that he was selfishly grabbing for acclaim. He was merely describing the nature and function of himself and the Holy Spirit in relation to God the Father. It is all part of the big plan.

To keep a correct balance, we need to honor and obey the Spirit (the Bible says not to "grieve" him or "put out his fire"). But we need to remember Paul's words in 1 Corinthians 2:12, "We have not received the Spirit of the world but the Spirit who is from God, that we may understand what God has given us"—salvation through Jesus Christ.

3

Love Serves

Has your boss ever offered to come home with you and wash your car? Has the mayor of your city ever raked your leaves, or your congressman done your dishes or scrubbed your toilet? People in authority over us—sometimes called public "servants"—rarely come to us and do our lowest, dirtiest jobs. Granted, they are busy doing other types of worthwhile service, but they hardly ever have contact with our lives.

Jesus is different. Although he is King of kings, he entered into personal service by healing, preaching, teaching, feeding. Jesus was aware of people's material needs, teaching extensively about money, but living without luxuries himself. But more than that, he gave sacrificially of himself in dealing with the needs of the total person—the body, mind, and spirit. He was the perfect servant, modeling for us the role we are to take. Like Jesus, we are to be servants.

A servant attitude

Philippians 2:5 strongly states the rationale for serving: "Your attitude should be the same as that of Christ Jesus: who, being in very nature God, did not consider equality with God something to be grasped, but made himself nothing, taking the very nature of a servant. . . . He humbled himself and became obedient to death—even death on a cross!"

There are several important ideas in this passage. Jesus' servanthood and ours stem from a correct attitude. He did not have to "grasp" or fight for status, power, freedom, or equality because they were already his. It is the same for us. Our position as a child of God with all its privileges is guaranteed when we believe in Jesus. Therefore, it is from this position of *strength* that we are enabled by the Holy Spirit to obey Christ and serve others, not from a position of weakness. John 13:3 says that "Jesus *knew* that the Father had put all things under his power, and that he had come from God and was returning to God." It was this knowledge, along with his great love, which enabled him to have a servant's heart.

So, being a servant does not mean that we go around dragging a ball and chain, taking abuse and suffering total lack of freedom. We are not coerced by God into slavery, but rather are privileged to serve as Christ did.

An upside-down kingdom

Shortly before Jesus' death, some of his disciples started to argue about who was going to rule with him. Jesus had spoken of setting up his kingdom, and the disciples were starting to vie for the best cabinet seats. Jesus very plainly outlined the criteria for his appointments: "You know that those who are regarded as rulers of the Gentiles lord it over them. . . . Not so with you. Instead, whoever wants to become great among you must be your servant, and whoever wants to be the first must be slave of all" (Mark 10:42-44. Also read Luke 22:24-30). What a blow to the disciples! Then, to illustrate what he meant, Jesus—the Lord of life—knelt down and washed each of the disciples' feet. He taught them servanthood by practicing it.

Paul, one of the greatest followers of Jesus, picked up on the servant idea in his life and writings. In Ephesians 2:10, he states one reason we are on earth: "We are God's workmanship, created in Christ Jesus to do good works." In the second letter to the

Corinthians, Paul called himself "your servant for Christ's sake" (4:5) and said, "I will very gladly spend for you everything I have and expend myself as well" (12:15). He urged the Roman Christians to make their lives, as he had, living sacrifices to God. That meant that their total being—every minute, every talent, every resource, every ounce of compassion—should be given to God to complete his purposes. Paul himself claimed to do this and then rejoice about it (Philippians 2:17). These are surely not the normal qualities and actions we associate with greatness. But they are, by God's standard.

A city on a hill

We must remember that our ability to serve—the strength, the correct attitude, the endurance, the humility, the vision—does not come from ourselves alone. It is God's Spirit who works in us to do every good thing. Therefore, we can "Stand firm . . . always [giving ourselves] fully to the work of the Lord, because [we] know that [our] labor in the Lord is not in vain" (1 Corinthians 15:58). When we serve, taking loving action on behalf of others, we are moving about as Christ's body—the Church—doing what he did while on earth.

Jesus said, "You are the light of the world. A city on a hill cannot be hidden. . . '. In the same way, let your light shine before men, that they may see your good deeds and praise your Father in heaven" (Matthew 5:14-16). The irony of servanthood is that it *does* exalt. We often receive no earthly reward whatsoever. But ultimately, in some place and time, our service becomes visible and highly honored. If some of that honor comes while we are still on earth, we have an obligation to direct people's attention away from ourselves to God and say something like, "This deed or service was done with God's help, for God. The credit goes to God. . . . By the way, do you know Jesus Christ? . . ." That was what Paul meant when he wrote, "And whatever you do, whether in word or deed, do it all in the name of the Lord Jesus, giving thanks to God the Father through him" (Colossians 3:17).

Jesus' claim on our lives is strong. Before his crucifixion, he said to his disciples, "Whoever serves me must follow me; and where I am, my servant also will be. My Father will honor the one who serves me" (John 12:26). Jesus was calling them to follow him, even to their death. The road of loving, caring service is often hard. It demands everything we have to give. But at the end of the road, we have the promise of life forever with Jesus in a place of high honor and joy. And, while on the journey, we have the satisfaction of knowing we are giving our best to God.

☑ Check It Out

1. According to Mark 10:45, why did Jesus come? _____

   _____

2. According to Ephesians 2:8-10, do good works save us? (a)

   _____ Why or why not? (b) _____

   _____

   _____

   (c) Why were we created? (v. 10) _____

3. Paul tells us in 2 Timothy 3:16-17 that one way we become "equipped" to do service for Jesus is by reading the _____.

4. What was Paul's reason in 1 Thessalonians 2:8 for sharing his life and the gospel message with the Thessalonians? _____

   _____

5. Paul says in Romans 12:1-2 that when we give ourselves totally in sacrifice to God's service, it is really a form of _____.

6. Servants of Christ are to show (a) _____ , and not become (b) _____. (Hebrews 6:11-12)

7. List from these Scriptures some things a servant does.
   (a) Romans 12:13 _____
   (b) Titus 3:14 _____
   _____
   (c) Colossians 4:12 _____
   (d) Matthew 25:31-36 _____
   _____
   _____
   (e) James 1:27 _____
   _____

 Talk It Over

1. Try to develop your own definition of a Christian servant.

2. Discuss whether you think this statement is true, and why: Doing charitable works *we* have chosen is good, but we are not really a servant until we are pressed by Christ into doing something we really would rather not do. (You may agree with some parts, and disagree with other portions of the sentence.)

continued on next page

3. Study Philippians 2:1-18. The writer, Paul, was literally in chains suffering humiliating circumstances.
   (a) Discuss what advice Paul gives to Christians.
   (b) Why do you think Paul could be hopeful, even though his Christian service had led to imprisonment?

4. Is it possible to be too proud of being humble? Explain. According to Colossians 3:17, what attitude is best when we serve?

5. List as many of the ways you can think of in which your local congregation and denomination act out their love in service to others. Discuss how you can become involved and put your love into action at home, in your community, in your congregation.

 # Up Close and Personal

Simon Peter the disciple. Read John 13:1-17.

1. What was Peter's reaction to Jesus washing his feet? Why?
2. What did Jesus mean in verse 8, "Unless I wash you, you have no part with me"?
3. Imagine that Jesus is asking you the question in verse 12. How would you answer?
4. Pray about finding some things God wants you to do to serve him. Have you asked God to take over every aspect of your life? Are you willing to follow God, no matter what he asks of you?

4

Love Gives

As we begin to recognize Jesus as the ultimate authority in our everyday lives, we learn that we need to involve him in everything we do, including the use of our money. Now, you may think that there is nothing particularly "spiritual" about money. We could justifiably spend a chapter on other topics. But Jesus did not avoid talking about money. In fact, the majority of his teachings had to do with material things. Jesus was very concerned about the relationship between our spiritual life and our material wealth.

Motivated by love

Aside from the time Jesus was on earth, he has been seated on the throne in heaven. For all eternity, he has enjoyed the splendor of all that is involved in ruling the universe. Yet, 2 Corinthians 8:9 says, "Though he was rich, he became poor so that you through his poverty might become rich." Only because Jesus laid aside all his privileges to become a person like you and me could we receive salvation by his death and resurrection.

We already know from John 3:16 that it was love that motivated God to do such an unselfish act. Likewise, it is God's love working in us through the Holy Spirit that leads Christians to unselfishly give of their lives and possessions. Yet it is clear from the number of biblical teachings on money that we wage a continual war with our old, selfish nature. The struggle involves how tightly we hold on to possessions and wealth, and whether we draw our security from things or from God.

Is wealth evil?

There is a common misquote that has gained popular acceptance: "Money is the root of all evil." People in the world often quote this statement tongue in cheek, yet blatantly go about accumulating all the wealth they can, in any way they can. Actually, the correct statement from 1 Timothy 6:10 is: "The *love* of money is a root of all kinds of evil." The verses go on to explain that when we replace God with money as our first love—and as our hope for security and happiness—we stray away from Christ and bring ourselves much grief.

Nowhere in the Bible does God say that our monetary system is bad. It allows us a way to convert our time and energy into an effective means of supplying our needs. (For example, instead of working for the grocer for our food, we work somewhere else for money which in turn buys the groceries.) What we tend to forget is that God owns everything. Our money and possessions are his; they are merely loaned to us to use for God's purposes. God created everything and declared it good. Possessions only become tinged with evil when they are the objects of greed and lust. Therefore, if we regard ourselves as overseers—or managers—of God's possessions, we are able to maintain a correct attitude. Then giving becomes a normal and natural expression of our gratitude to God for his love and provision for us.

How can I get along if I give my money away?

We live in a society that puts great value on possessions. It is almost inconceivable to us not to own certain things that seem to give us worldly respectability and comfort. We tend to surround ourselves with things that give us the illusion of security. Many of us earn more and more, and spend more and more, not giving any thought to how unnecessarily extravagant our lifestyle has become. We have a lot, but we often think we have very little.

For others of us, when the rent, the utilities, the food, the car, and the clothes are paid for, there seldom is much or any left over. Where would money come from to give to the church or to meet other people's needs? And aren't we supposed to save a little in case of emergencies or for old age so we don't become a burden to anyone?

Believe it or not, God understands all these things, and he wants us to work for our money and be responsible with it, taking care of our families and our debts. But time after time, Jesus gave such warnings as, "Watch out! Be on your guard against all kinds of greed; a man's life does not consist in the abundance of his possessions." In the sixth chapter of Matthew, Jesus pleaded with his followers not to worry about food or clothes, saying that seeking God's kingdom (obeying God) is far more important than these. He said, "Do not store up treasures on earth, where moth and rust destroy, and where thieves break in and steal. . . . Store up . . . treasures in heaven. . . . For where your treasure is, there your heart will be also."

Treasure in heaven

There is absolutely no doubt from Scripture that giving will be rewarded. God says in Malachi 3:10, "See if I will not throw open the floodgates of heaven and pour out so much blessing that you will not have room for it." God does not ignore our sacrifices. "God is not unjust; he will not forget your work and the love you have shown him as you have helped his people" (Hebrews 6:10). Many Bible passages speak of God's faithfulness to those who invest in God's work instead of their own desires for profit. There is little doubt that we are recipients of many of God's blessings while we are on earth. God has promised to provide all we *need* (not necessarily all we want).

However, some blessings will be reserved for us in heaven. People sometimes fall into a trap by thinking that all we need to do to have material prosperity is to give. They misguidedly give to the church, thinking that they'll miraculously come into money to get them out of debt, to buy a new TV, or to salvage a business. Surely God can and does provide miracles in our finances, but only when our motivation is right, or when it suits God's purposes. We can't "buy" God's blessing.

This misunderstanding is no new problem. The Apostle Paul, nearly 2,000 years ago, said that some people believe "godliness is a means to financial gain." Correcting that misconception, he adds, "But godliness with contentment is great gain. For we brought nothing into the world, and we can take nothing out of it" (1 Timothy 6:5-6).

So, how should I give?

Find out about needs. According to Peter, "Each one should use whatever gift he has received to serve others, faithfully administering God's grace in its various forms" (1 Peter 4:10). This statement is not limited to, but does include, money. We are to give according to what has been given us. Since the money we have isn't truly our own, we are to give generously when we see there are needs.

Some people barricade themselves in their secure, tidy world and don't allow themselves to come in contact with need. That is one of the best reasons for getting involved in our neighborhood and in our local church. There are needs all around. But if we don't allow ourselves to be put in a position to know about them, our hearts of compassion are not stirred. It is possible to insulate ourselves against the discomfort of the Holy Spirit's proddings to do something about needs. But in doing so, we also deprive ourselves of the blessings.

Plan your giving. Paul instructs the believers in 1 Corinthians 16:2, "On the first day of the week, . . . set aside a sum of money in keeping with [your] income, saving it up." This is similar to the Old Testament practice of the tithe—taking one tenth of earnings (before taxes!) and putting it aside before paying the bills and fulfilling our wants. That way, we are sure to have it to give. Many people give much more than a tenth of their income and still live modestly and well. Others start with a smaller amount and create a plan to gradually increase their giving by a certain percentage each year. Generally speaking, the tithe is the minimum a Christian should strive to give.

Remember this: Whoever sows sparingly will also reap sparingly, and whoever sows generously will also reap generously.

2 Corinthians 9:6

Give without a grudging heart. Second Corinthians 9:7 says that "God loves a cheerful giver." It is the condition of our heart when we give that God delights in. If we resent giving, or give under compulsion, God is not happy. If we hold back, knowing through the Spirit's advice that we can and should give more, God is not pleased, and we cannot be cheerful. But often when we take a step of faith and sacrificially go beyond what we think we can afford, God is pleased and gives us joy.

Be compassionate, but wise. Sometimes it's not the TV preacher, or the United Way, or other world-run organizations that need your offerings the most. These might be O.K. But at times it's the unlovable neighbor down the street who needs to see God through you as you provide for a certain need. Sometimes it's the person in the church pew next to you who has accumulated medical bills. Other times, it's a missionary in Japan or Venezuela who is trying to be self-supporting while giving out the good news far away. Perhaps it's the church administrator or pastor who lives a day-to-day subsistence or whose children can't have a college education because he is serving the Lord. Many needs such as these are cared for by giving to the budget of your local congregation. But your love may motivate you to go beyond your tithe to the church to meet such needs.

Trust the local church. Your local congregation most likely has a budget which has been agreed upon by the members after much prayer, work, and planning by the leaders. Participation in a local church gives us opportunity to reach into areas of need that are beyond the scope of personal, direct giving. We are not always totally aware of the results of our giving when we put our money into the offering plate on Sunday. Yet as we trust those

Tips on giving

1. Many churches have a confidential system of offering envelopes. If you see people putting such an envelope in the offering plate as it is passed, ask your pastor whether the church treasurer will issue you some also. As you prayerfully prepare to give before you come to church, you can use the envelopes. This way you don't end up being embarrassed as you dig last minute into your pocket or purse when the offering plate comes to your aisle. Of course, you don't *need* an envelope to give!
2. Don't compare what you give to others. Instead, read Scripture about giving, and listen to and obey the Holy Spirit. Giving is between you and the Lord.
3. Give in the sight of your children. They will learn to be giving people, too.
4. Ask to see the church budget and learn where your money is going. Be interested. You will be excited to see how your money is working for God's purposes.
5. If you feel led to give to a Christian organization outside your denomination, check with your pastor. There are ways to find out whether the organization is submitting to measures of financial accountability set up by the Christian community.

who put our dollars to work either in the local church, the community, or at the denominational level, we can be satisfied our money is being carefully handled to honor God's great purposes.

Giving is one of the best ways to put your love in action. God gave us the supreme, unselfish gift in Jesus Christ and continues to bless us. God is great and worthy of more than "a tip." In addition, Jesus asks us to give up anything that keeps us from putting all our love and trust in him. Sometimes that is our possessions.

☑ Check It Out

1. Read Deuteronomy 8:17-18. (a) What mistake do we some-times make in thinking about our money? _____

   _____

   (b) Who gives you the ability and strength to earn money?

   _____

2. Read 1 John 3:17. What is lacking in us if we don't do what we can about the needs we are aware of? _____

3. Read Isaiah 58:10-11. In your own words, what is the result of "spending yourselves in behalf of the hungry, and satisfying the needs of the oppressed"? _____

4. How are we to give, according to Matthew 6:3-4? _____

   _____ .

5. What does Paul call our giving in the last part of Philippians 4:18? _____

_____

6. According to Matthew 25:34-40, whom are you really serving when you help other people? _____ (If you have time, skim all of Chapters 24—26:1-2 to gain a better understanding of this passage.)

7. Read Matthew 6:25-33. What promise is given in Matthew 6:33 to those who don't worry about "things," but do first what pleases God? _____

 Talk It Over

1. How is it possible for a poor person to have a bad attitude about riches? (Read Exodus 20:17; and 1 Timothy 6:9-10.)

2. What was the rich man's foolish mistake in Luke 12:16-21? What does it mean to be "rich toward God"? Are all people bad who have money?

3. What has been your attitude toward money in the past? What two or three ideas in this chapter were new to you?

4. What difference will your new-found faith in Christ mean to you in terms of simplifying your lifestyle ("living more on less")? What specific things could you do to make better use of your money for God?

Up Close and Personal

The Rich Young Man. Read Matthew 19:16-26.

1. What kept this man from following Jesus?
2. Did the man know what he should do?
3. Why didn't Jesus tell him just to give away a tithe (one tenth) of what he owned?

The poor widow. Read Mark 12:41-44.

1. In what sense had the widow put more into the treasury than all the others?
2. Do you think the widow went hungry that week?
3. What amount would constitute "sacrificial giving" for you?

Zacchaeus. Read Luke 19:1-10.

1. Was Zacchaeus able to buy salvation by giving to the poor?
2. Why did Zacchaeus give away his possessions and pay back those he had cheated (called "restitution")?
3. Have you ever experienced great joy in helping someone in need? Explain.

5

Love Restores

Once we have the desire to love, to serve, and to give, we will find ourselves thrust more and more into relationships with people, both Christian and non-Christian. Although God knows that personal interaction is not always easy, God calls most of us to deal daily with other people—whether at home, in the church or community, or on the job. God is concerned about peace in those relationships, desiring that people live and work together in harmony. In the Bible, we find guidance for good relationships. But nothing is of more help than understanding how God took action to restore his own loving relationship with mankind.

God's permanent love

Did you ever wonder why God hasn't given up on humanity—on you and me? Human beings sin and continually ignore and hurt God, despite his great love and provision for us. God is a just God, so why has he continued to love us?

God is committed to his creation. God has modeled for us by his actions throughout human history that we can't give up when things go wrong. People are God's priority. We are special to God, worth all the suffering Jesus bore, so that we could have a right relationship with God. Sin wasn't God's fault. God justifiably could have given up on us, but that's not the case. Nor should it be with us in our relationships. People are important. Even when we are not at fault, we need to pursue healing instead of letting the hurt remain final.

Brokenness is not the end. Have you ever been in such a difficult situation with a person that you finally broke the relationship? You went your separate ways, possibly never seeing each other again. When this happens, there is often bitterness and hatred. Sick feelings of guilt and loneliness from such unresolved conflicts leave us empty and may linger with us the rest of our lives. Relationships have a way of being lasting—either by bringing permanent happiness or permanent scars.

But God's plan for living, carefully followed, is a blueprint for wholeness and happiness. If we know and obey the commands in Scripture, if we follow the counsel of the Holy Spirit and our friends in the church, God provides us the wisdom and guidance we need to know how to create and maintain, as well as restore, peaceful relationships. God does not want brokenness to be the final outcome. The desire of God's heart is peace, reconciliation, and wholeness in relationships.

Godly love is a decision. Romans 5:8 explains, "You see, at just the right time, when we were still powerless, Christ died for the ungodly [us!]. Very rarely will anyone die for a righteous man, though for a good man someone might possibly dare to die. But God demonstrates his own love for us in this: While we were still sinners, Christ died for us."

God had nothing to gain by the death of his Son except for the possibility of reconciliation—the restoring of a peaceful relationship—with each of us. It was a daring risk, since the choice of believing in Jesus is still up to us. God's love is not merely a feeling; it is a conscious decision to act on behalf of the unlovely and unlovable. God's love took the form of premeditated, chosen action. That is the highest form of love—the kind of love we now have an obligation and opportunity to exercise in our personal relationships.

Love's plan for restoration

Forgiveness. People who have received salvation in Jesus Christ have begun to understand the meaning of forgiveness. We each had to come to God, realizing and confessing our own sin, before we could be reunited with God as one of his children. Gratefully we ran into God's arms, and accepted his forgiveness. Scripture tells us our sins are to God as if they had never happened. That is how completely God forgives.

Yet, we are not normally as generous, are we? Forgiveness often comes hard. Stuck in our old human tendencies, we tend to hold onto a grudge. Or we outwardly forgive, but inwardly punish that person, looking for a way to retaliate. So our hatred burns within us, destroying us as well as our relationship with the other person. But Jesus taught that we will experience forgiveness in proportion to our forgiveness of others. If people hurt us over and over, we are to forgive them over and over, just as God forgives us when we confess our sins (1 John 1:7-9).

Mutual respect. One of the hardest commands in Scripture is the one which says, "Do nothing out of selfish ambition or vain conceit, but in humility consider others better than yourselves" (Philippians 2:3). We live in a society which teaches winning as the highest goal; selfish ambition as the way to success; and the accumulation of possessions and praise at the expense of other persons. But God has a different way, which he showed us in Jesus.

As we have learned in the previous chapters, Jesus had every right to act as supreme ruler, but he laid aside that right in order to serve and die. The same motivation needs to permeate our relationships. Time and again Jesus called on his disciples to love—even their enemies. If someone compels you to walk a mile with him, Jesus said to walk two. If someone insults us, we are to proceed without retaliation, even taking a courageous, aggressive role in reestablishing harmony with the other person. We are to take on the role of peacemaker in difficult situations. Not only did Jesus teach these things, he did them. And not only does he command them of us, but God sent the Holy Spirit to empower his people to do them.

Power in the Church. Christians are called by God to apply these principles in their personal lives. In addition, the Church—the combined body of believers—often plays an active role in creating harmony. Inside the church body, leaders function as mediators in disputes. In chapter 18 of Matthew, we find guidelines for gently restoring people to fellowship who have been in the wrong. Moreover, at the denominational level, many churches are participating in peacemaking on a worldwide scale, intervening in countries where warring factions need the resources of love, sacrifice, hope, and assistance that the Church uniquely can offer.

Love's privilege

In case you feel, in the light of all that has been said, that you are expected to become cowardly and weak, take heart. Remember that God's formula entailing love and servanthood has

> *All of you, live in harmony with one another; be sympathetic, love as brothers, be compassionate and humble. Do not repay evil with evil or insult with insult, but with blessing, because to this you were called so that you may inherit a blessing. For "Whoever would love life and see good days must keep his tongue from evil and his lips from deceitful speech. He must turn from evil and do good; he must seek peace and pursue it."*
>
> *1 Peter 3:8-11*

contentment and blessing on the other side of the equal sign. What may appear to the world as weakness, actually may be the greatest strength. It usually takes more courage and power to make peace than to sustain conflict.

God does not set out to demean us. Quite the opposite. Our lives can never be more exalted than when they display the love of Christ; they are never more attractive than when we share the example of Christ. The greatest glory is to reflect the glory of

Tips for troubled relationships

1. Begin with prayer. Ask God to reveal to you in what ways you have contributed to the misunderstanding. Ask God to give you a heart full of love and forgiveness.
2. Read Matthew 18. Decide on a proper course of action. Once the plan is known, go about doing it with calm assurance of God's power and presence.
3. Share with the other person how you perceive the situation and try to talk it out. Or if confrontation is not necessary, continue to show love and concern for the person. Don't withdraw.
4. If it becomes necessary to involve someone else in the process, go to your pastor or a mature third person to help each of you better listen to the other. Trust the wisdom of the Scriptures and the mediators involved.
5. Realize that disagreements—even within the church—are normal. While some conflicts are "spiritual" and involve God's truth, many are "human" and can be tolerated and worked through in the context of Christian patience and love.

Christ. The call to peace is our privilege—one that God has freely extended to all who will obey him.

If you follow God's formula for right relationships, as found in the Bible and as directed by the Holy Spirit and the Church, you will discover that God's way is right. Granted, God's timing may be different from ours. Often God works either slower or faster than we would wish to make things right between us and other people. Yet, as we patiently cooperate with God, not imposing our own time limits on people and situations, God works to create the right outcome.

Romans 8:28 and 31-32 says, "We know that in all things God works for the good of those who love him, who have been called according to his purpose. . . . What, then, shall we say in response to this? If God is for us, who can be against us? He who did not spare his own Son, but gave him up for us all—how will he not also, along with him, graciously give us all things?" Even peace in our relationships.

☑ Check It Out

1. Read Isaiah 53, the entire chapter. (The "he" in the chapter refers to Jesus.)

   (a) How many of us have wandered (before salvation) away from God, stupidly following our own plans instead of God's? _____

   (b) What was God's plan to save us, according to verses 4-5, 10-11? _____

   _____

   (c) Why do you think God did what he did? _____

   _____

2. The word "reconciled" is found in all these verses: Romans 5:10; 2 Corinthians 5:18-20; Ephesians 2:13-16; Colossians 1:19-20. After reading them all, write down in your own words what you have learned about being reconciled to God and to other people: _____

_____

_____

_____

3. The Sermon on the Mount, given by Jesus and recorded in Matthew 5—7, gives many guidelines for good relationships. Skim the three chapters, then go back and put into your own words some of the tough commandments of Jesus:

   (a) Matthew 5:21-22 _____

   (b) Matthew 5:23-24 _____

   (c) Matthew 5:27-30 _____

4. What do these verses say to us about our conduct with other people, primarily those within the church?

   (a) Romans 14:19 _____

   _____

   (b) Romans 15:7 _____

   _____

   (c) 1 Corinthians 12:25 _____

   (d) Galatians 6:2 _____

   (e) Ephesians 4:1-2 _____

   _____

   (f) Ephesians 5:21 _____

(g) Colossians 3:9 _____

(h) Colossians 3:13, 16 _____

(i) 1 Thessalonians 4:18 _____

(j) James 4:11 _____

(k) James 5:16 _____

(l) 1 Peter 5:5 _____

5. List the qualities of love from 1 Corinthians 13:4-8: _____

_____

_____

_____

_____

 # Talk It Over

1. Was there anything new to you about the definition of God's love on page 39? (". . . a conscious decision to act on behalf of the unlovely and unlovable . . . premeditated, chosen action.") Explain.

2. Have you ever experienced a broken relationship? Would you handle that situation differently now that you are a Christian? What guidelines, principles, and promises do you find in Matthew, chapter 18?

3. Name a person you have a difficult time getting along with now. Ask yourself these questions:
   (a) Does God want me to keep trying? Why?
   (b) What have I or the other person done or said that requires my forgiveness?

continued on next page

(c) Should I forgive before he/she asks? What if they never ask?

(d) What are that person's good qualities? How is he/she valuable in God's eyes?

(e) Will I exercise my God-given power to love that person?

4. Take a few minutes to pray together, asking God to work out the difficult relationships in your life. Ask the Holy Spirit to enter into those situations, changing the persons in them (including you) for the good. Thank God that he cares for you and is going to help you.

5. Talk about your church's participation in peacemaking around the world. To your knowledge, what is the body of Christ doing to promote peace?

 # Up Close and Personal

Jacob and Esau reconcile. Read Genesis 32:3-21; and Genesis 33:1-20. (As background to this passage, you need to know that years before, the younger brother Jacob had stolen his older brother Esau's inheritance. Jacob left home. Now they are preparing to meet again.)

1. In this case, which person took the initiative to mend the relationship—the injured or the one who inflicted injury? What indications are there that Jacob was afraid of what Esau's response might be?

2. How did Jacob prepare for the meeting? What was Esau's response? (Note especially 33:4-5, 9.) What if Esau had not responded so well to Jacob's initiative? Did Jacob do the right thing? What was Jacob's response to God when it was all over (33:18-20)?

3. In mending your troubled relationships, consider the role that prayer, humility, offers of restitution, and honoring God have in the action you take.

6

Love Prepares

Are you aware that you are preparing for a great wedding? One very exciting and important day, Christ will return to see you and every other member of the Church throughout the ages coming together to unite with him forever. In a triumphant moment, with Christ as the groom and the Church as the bride, we will confirm our love—Christ's love for us, and ours for him.

This marriage will not be like many of those of the world in which vows are broken, and in which divorce or disillusionment tear apart our dreams for happiness. This marriage is the permanent binding together of the perfect Christ with his pure and spotless bride. It is a real moment which we need to anxiously await, preparing ourselves in every detail. It is precisely because we look for Christ to return to earth for his bride that we are careful how we live—in purity, in unity, and in joy.

Stay in the light

According to the Bible, people who don't have Jesus live in darkness. This is a metaphor which means being associated with and controlled by evil and wrongdoing—sin. But Christians are to be "children of light" (Ephesians 5:8-11). Verse 11 says, "Have nothing to do with the fruitless deeds of darkness, but rather expose them." Whether we like it or not, and whether or not we *say* a single word, our lives and our right living will be like spotlights that shine brightly on the ungodly deeds of others. People who do wrong don't like having their lives exposed for all to see. Yet that is what we do when we are around them, simply because we are who we now are—Christians. While some people will welcome the light of our presence in their lives, others without the Lord often would rather see our Christian glow snuffed out.

It is interesting that in many Bible passages which list sinful acts (see Check It Out, Question 1), there is an immediate mention of judgment and condemnation. The Bible is quite clear that some people will be denied entrance into God's kingdom and be out of God's presence forever because of their willful, habitual sinfulness. Aware of this fact, we need to ask the Holy Spirit to empower us with everything we need to live right in the midst of a sinful world—whether it be at home or at work or play. Remembering that the Spirit is stronger than anything the world can toss our way, we will be able to follow the counsel of Scripture, and wisely decide whom to be with and what to do.

Sometimes we will need to flee certain situations. Other times, we will want to stand our ground with the Lord at our side. God wants us to love people—all people—but not to be part of the wrong they might do. This may mean a struggle, especially in the first years of our Christian life, when the consequences of our old life are still running their course. But God does not ask anything of us without giving us the strength and wisdom to do it. God can give us the ability to live in the midst of a sinful world, yet not be a part of its actions and attitudes.

Put on the "armor"

One of the most graphic Bible passages is Ephesians 6:13-17. The writer says that the pressures—the attacks—on our spiritual lives can be so strong that we should put on Christian "armor" (a belt of truth; breastplate of righteousness; on our feet, the gospel of peace; the shield of faith; the helmet of salvation; and the sword of the Spirit which is the Word of God). Even though this may conjure up a humorous picture of a medieval knight, the message

Prepare your minds for action; be self-controlled; set your hope fully on the grace to be given you when Jesus Christ is revealed. As obedient children, do not conform to the evil desires you had when you lived in ignorance. But just as he who called you is holy, so be holy in all you do.

1 Peter 1:13-16

is that we must be fully aware of and prepared for spiritual battle. Sometimes the struggle against sin is as violent and obvious as war.

Other times, the path into sin is camouflaged with good intentions, flowery words, or apparent success. Paul warns, " 'Everything is permissible for me'—but not everything is beneficial" (see 1 Corinthians 6:12-20). We are free in Christ to do many things, but they may not all be good for us. It is sometimes easy to take our eyes away from Jesus and lose the correct path and focus for our lives. Not only do we need to watch out for those influences which cause us to blatantly sin, but we need to live positive lives, growing in goodness, knowledge, self-control, perseverance, godliness, kindness, and love, which "will keep [us] from being ineffective and unproductive" in our Christian lives (2 Peter 1:5-8).

Renew your mind

The Apostle Paul gives us good advice in Romans 12:2: "Do not conform any longer to the pattern of this world, but be transformed by the renewing of your mind. Then you will be able to test and approve what God's will is." Paul knew that pressures to conform to the non-believing world around us would be hard to bear. So he told us to keep our minds focused on Jesus. "Set your hearts on things above, where Christ is seated at the right hand of God. Set your minds on things above, not on earthly things" (Colossians 3:2). Paul also warned against being taken "captive" by wrong ways of thinking which are based on "human tradition and the basic traditions of this world rather than on Christ" (Colossians 2:8). It is possible to remain free in Christ. By reading the Bible and good Christian literature, praying, and developing close ties in Sunday school and study groups with other Christians in the church, a Christian can keep his or her mind focused on the right things.

You may be finding it necessary to make some important decisions involving your daily habits and the people with whom you associate. There is no doubt that the people we spend time with have a great effect on what we think about and whether we are obedient to Jesus' commands. Thus, we are warned in Scripture not to "yoke" ourselves with non-Christians in new business relationships, marriage, or other extremely close associations. (Of course, if you are married to a non-Christian, you will want to do all you can to stay in that relationship as a witness to God's unfailing love.) On the advice of your pastor and the Holy Spirit, you may decide that you need to disentangle yourself from people who are having a harmful influence on you and the people you love. On the other hand, you may feel you are strongly enough grounded in your Christian life to go ahead and spend time with certain people. You will not want to participate with them anymore in wrong acts. But you may feel you can begin to influence them to become Christians by your continued contact.

Cling to the Church

On the night before his crucifixion, a night filled with terror and fear, Jesus prayed long and earnestly for all believers—then and since. He asked God the Father to protect them from evil, and to set them apart from the world as his special people. He also pleaded for them to be "brought to complete unity" so people will know that he is the Christ, the only Savior. Earlier, at his last supper with the disciples before his death, Jesus told them to remember him every time they ate and drank together. He wanted them to feel his very blood coursing through their veins, and his own body meshed with theirs.

Because we are this closely bonded to Christ today as well, we are therefore linked with one another—one body, one bride. Paul used another word picture. He called us "fellow citizens with God's people and members of God's household, built on the foundation of the apostles and prophets, with Christ Jesus himself as the cornerstone. In him the whole building is joined together and rises to become a holy temple in the Lord" (Ephesians 2:19-21). It is easy to imagine ourselves as one of the supporting bricks, with God's love as the mortar.

Although our unity in Christ is established in *fact* when we become a Christian, it only becomes *evident* as we live each day with Christ as Lord. It is utterly impossible for us to choose to be separate from the church in our daily lives and still remain obedient to Christ's wishes. We must cling to the Lord in our personal faith. But we are also called to hold fast to the church. If we don't, we grieve Christ, the one who prayed for us to be one, and who died to accomplish it.

Finish the race

You made a decision when you said you would follow Christ. By now you are becoming aware of the implications of that decision for your day-to-day life. Moreover, each day God is working in you, changing you to be more and more like Christ. By now you have probably realized that it is possible to stand in the way of that process by trying to hold onto parts of your life that are not pleasing to God.

The writer of Hebrews knew this when he advised, "Throw off everything that hinders and the sin that so easily entangles, and let us run with perseverance the race marked out for us" (12:1). Can you picture a marathon runner in the middle of a race suddenly encountering a net thrown in his path? Nothing he does, no amount of energy, will release him to continue the race until he is cut out of the net. Sometimes the habits and associations from our pre-Christian world are like that net. It takes the power of Christ to cut us free.

We began this book with a discussion of freedom, and that is where we will end it. Our life with God means we have freedom and power to love, to serve, to give, and to enjoy God forever. Little by little—as you grow, change, are tested, love, and grow some more—your life will be flooded with the light of God's presence. Then, one glorious day, you will meet Jesus face to face. That will be worth every problem, every moment of confusion, every spiritual battle, every struggle with physical pain. Like runners in a marathon race, you will feel the exhilaration and the victory as you complete the course God has mapped out for you.

None of us has any idea whether we will die before Christ's return. But we must live every day together in purity, unity, and harmony as if he will come today. As we continue in our Christian walk to keep our eyes on the final outcome of our faith, which is everlasting life, we have assurance that we will someday be with Jesus as his bride. Many things—good and bad—will happen to us along the way. We can choose to quit, to be captives of discouraged, inactive, unhelpful lives. Or we can choose the victorious freedom of knowing, loving, and following God more closely each day.

God desires for us active, useful, fruitful lives. God wants to see us put our love in action!

The insights you have gained in Life With God: Basics for New Christians *and this book are only a beginning. Now you will want to continue to take action because of what you've learned. Plan a strategy of continued Bible study. Become a faithful and involved attender in your local congregation. If you have not already done so, consult with your pastor about baptism and church membership. Experience and share the riches of God's love.*

☑ Check It Out

Be sure to do the questions in this chapter. Don't miss the special privilege of reading and learning directly from God's Word.

1. (a) List the sins of darkness from Galatians 5:19-21; 1 Thessalonians 4:3-6; 2 Thessalonians 1:8-9; and Colossians 3:5-9:

_____

_____

_____

_____

_____

(b) Summarize the results: _____

_____

_____

2. Sometimes we need to "come out" from among non-Christians and be (a) _____ (2 Corinthians 6:17). Other times, we must be Christ's (b) _____ in the world (2 Corinthians 5:20).

3. Philippians 4:8-9 has good guidelines for what to focus our thoughts and attention on. Read these verses and put them in your own words:

_____

_____

_____

_____

4. Write down in your own words what will happen (a) to those who die (fall asleep) before Christ's return, and (b) to those still alive at his return (1 Thessalonians 4:13-18).

(a) _____

_____

(b) _____

_____

_____

5. What does Matthew 24:36-44 tell us about Christ's return?
(a) How will the world be acting when he comes? (verses 37-39) _____

_____

(b) What instructions does this passage give Christians? (verses 42, 44) _____

_____

6. Read 1 Thessalonians 5:1-11. List some things we should do to be prepared for Christ's return: _____

_____

_____

7. What are some of the bits of parting advice the writer of Hebrews gives to his readers? All the verses are from Chapter 13:
(a) v. 1 _____

(b) v. 2 _____

(c) v. 3 _____

(d) v. 4 _____

(e) v. 5 _____

(f) v. 7 _____

(g) v. 9 _____

(h) v. 15 _____

(i) v. 16 _____

(j) v. 17 _____

(k) v. 18 _____

 Talk It Over

1. Spend some time talking about Jesus' return. How do you feel about it? How will you live differently now that you know he will return? Are you ready?

2. Talk about some of the subtle habits and influences that may be keeping you from being a productive and growing person in Jesus Christ. Take time to pray together for the empowering of the Holy Spirit to help you claim victory in these areas.

3. Read and discuss the parable of the ten virgins in Matthew 25:1-13. Will there come a time when it is too late to follow

Jesus? What persons do you know who need to hear the message of salvation? Will you tell them?

4. Talk about your impressions of the word "holy." Does it have good or bad connotations for you? What does "holy" seem to mean in the Bible? Read these Scripture passages to find out:

   Leviticus 20:7-8   2 Corinthians 7:1
   Colossians 1:21-22 and 3:12 Ephesians 1:4 and 4:22-24
   1 Timothy 2:8   2 Timothy 1:9

5. Discuss what to do next. Consider asking your pastor if you may join a membership class in your church. What will be your next steps in study? in giving and service? in fellowship? in your prayer life?

 # Up Close and Personal

Paul finishes the race. Read Philippians 1:12-14 and 19-26; Philippians 3:1-21; and 2 Timothy 4:6-8.

1. What statements in these passages indicate that Paul believes his death is near? What is his attitude about death? about life?

2. What did Paul intend to do until the end of his earthly life? What warnings and advice does he give?

3. How would your attitudes and actions compare to Paul's if you knew you would soon meet Jesus face to face? Do you intend to be able to say that you have "fought the good fight," "finished the race," and "kept the faith"?

*May God himself, the God of peace, sanc-
tify you through and through. May your
whole spirit, soul and body be kept blameless
at the coming of our Lord Jesus Christ. The
one who calls you is faithful and he will do
it. . . . The Spirit and the Bride say,
"Come!" . . . Amen. Come, Lord Jesus.*

Ephesians 3:20-21 and Revelation 22:17, 20

Six-Week Bible Reading Plan

Life with God: Basics for New Christians contained three two-week Bible reading plans about the life and teachings of Jesus, the plan of salvation, and various prayers in the Bible. Here are three more two-week plans for reading the Bible.

Two weeks on the life and teachings of Paul
☐ Day 1. Acts 9: The conversion of Saul.
☐ Day 2. Acts 16: Paul's Macedonian call and a jailbreak.
☐ Day 3. Acts 17: Scenes from Paul's missionary journeys.
☐ Day 4. Acts 26: Paul tells his life story to a king.
☐ Day 5. Acts 27: Shipwreck on the way to Rome.
☐ Day 6. Acts 28: Paul's arrival in Rome.
☐ Day 7. Romans 3: Paul's theology in a nutshell.
☐ Day 8. Romans 7: Struggle with sin.
☐ Day 9. Romans 8: Life in the Spirit.
☐ Day 10. 1 Corinthians 13: Paul's description of love.
☐ Day 11. 1 Corinthians 15: Thoughts on the afterlife.
☐ Day 12. Galatians 5: Freedom in Christ.
☐ Day 13. Ephesians 3: Paul's summary of his mission.
☐ Day 14. Philippians 2: Imitating Christ.

Two weeks on the Holy Spirit
☐ Day 1. Judges 14: Giving strength to Samson.
☐ Day 2. 1 Samuel 10: King Saul's experience.
☐ Day 3. Matthew 3:1—4:10: Role in Jesus' baptism and temptation.
☐ Day 4. John 14: Jesus promises the Spirit.
☐ Day 5. John 16: The work of the Spirit.
☐ Day 6. Acts 2: Coming of the Spirit at Pentecost.
☐ Day 7. Acts 10: Guidance to Peter on accepting Gentiles.
☐ Day 8. Romans 8: Christians' victory in the Spirit.
☐ Day 9. 1 Corinthians 2: Wisdom from the Spirit.
☐ Day 10. 1 Corinthians 12: Gifts of the Spirit.
☐ Day 11. 1 Corinthians 14: Gifts of tongues and prophecy.
☐ Day 12. Galatians 5: Life in the Spirit.
☐ Day 13. Ephesians 4: Unity and gifts.
☐ Day 14. 1 John 4: Signs of the Spirit.

Two weeks on social justice

- ☐ Day 1. Exodus 3: God hears the cries of the slaves.
- ☐ Day 2. Leviticus 25: The Year of Jubilee, when economics even out.
- ☐ Day 3. Ruth 2: A poor woman finds help.
- ☐ Day 4. 1 Kings 21: Elijah speaks to a land-grabbing, murderous king.
- ☐ Day 5. Nehemiah 5: Nehemiah demands justice for the poor.
- ☐ Day 6. Isaiah 5: Woe to fun-loving materialists.
- ☐ Day 7. Isaiah 58: Worship that God appreciates.
- ☐ Day 8. Jeremiah 34: Freedom for slaves.
- ☐ Day 9. Amos 2: Sins against God by his own people.
- ☐ Day 10. Amos 6: Woe to the complacent.
- ☐ Day 11. Micah 6: What the Lord requires.
- ☐ Day 12. Luke 3: John the Baptist tells how to prepare for Jesus.
- ☐ Day 13. Matthew 6: Jesus speaks on material things.
- ☐ Day 14. James 2: Favoring the rich, showing compassion for the poor.

Reprinted by permission from *The Student Bible: New International Version,* published by Zondervan Bible Publishers, Grand Rapids, Michigan.

Other two-week tracks are available in *The Student Bible.* This Bible also lists a six-month track; an overview of the entire Bible; and a three-year track, to read all the way through the Bible.

Prayer Journal

These pages are provided for you to list your prayer requests and the answers. Also list praises.

Date	*Prayers and praises*	*Date and Answer*

Date   *Prayers and praises*   *Date and Answer*

Answers

(taken from the New International Version)

Chapter 1

1. (a) Teacher, Lord
   (b) Lord, Christ
   (c) King of kings, Lord of lords
   (d) Lord of the dead and the living
2. that those who live shall no longer live for themselves, but for him
3. (a) seated at the right hand of the Father
   (b) exalted in the highest place/ every one will honor him
4. (a) trust in the Lord with all your heart
   (b) lean not on your own understanding
   (c) in all your ways acknowledge him
   (d) he will make your paths straight (direct your paths)
5. discipline (Discipline here means more than punishment. It involves the entire area of guidance, teaching, and correction of our course, which God has various ways of accomplishing.)
6. God will teach and counsel us in what we should do, and watch over us
7. If we connect our purposes with Christ's, he will share the work with us and lighten our load.
8. love with actions and in truth
9. (a) faith
   (b) actions
10. obeying

Chapter 2

1. G   Acts 1:8
    C   Acts 4:31
    K   Acts 9:31
    I   1 Corinthians 3:16
    M   Ephesians 4:3
    E   Ephesians 1:13-14
    F   John 14:26
    B   John 15:26-27
    A   John 16:8-11
    J   Romans 5:5
    D   Romans 8:6
    L   Romans 15:17-19
    H   1 John 4:4
2. love, joy, peace, patience, kindness, goodness, faithfulness, gentleness, self-control, compassion, humility, forgiveness, faith, knowledge, perseverance, godliness

Chapter 3

1. to serve and give his life as a ransom for many
2. (a) no
   (b) it is by grace we are saved, through faith—and it is the gift of God—not works, so that no one can boast
   (c) to do good works
3. Scriptures
4. He loved them.
5. worship
6. (a) diligence
   (b) lazy
7. (a) shares with God's people who are in need; provides hospitality
   (b) devotes him or herself to doing good; provides for daily necessities; does not have an unproductive life
   (c) wrestles in prayer

(d) feeds the hungry; gives drink to the thirsty; gives hospitality to strangers; clothes the needy; looks after the sick; visits those in prison

(e) looks after orphans and widows; keeps oneself pure

Chapter 4

1. (a) My power and strength have produced this wealth for me.
   (b) God
2. the love of God
3. God will guide and bless us
4. in secret
5. a fragrant offering, an acceptable sacrifice, pleasing to God
6. Jesus (He *is* the King in the story he is telling the disciples.)
7. All these things [our basic needs] will be given to you.

Chapter 5

1. (a) all of us
   (b) Jesus carried our sin and weaknesses in his own body and was punished and suffered in our place.
   (c) He loves us and therefore created a plan whereby we could make peace with God.
2. We can rejoice that it is through Jesus we can be reconciled to God. We are to give this message of reconciliation to others. Because we have peace with God, we also have peace with all other believers.

3. (a) murder comes from anger in the heart; harbored anger is wrong
   (b) our offerings aren't pleasing to God if we have strife in our relationships
   (c) don't even look lustfully at a person, much less commit adultery; sin comes from the heart—it is possible to sin without *doing* anything.
4. (a) make every effort to do what leads to peace and mutual edification
   (b) accept one another, as Christ accepted you, in order to bring praise to God
   (c) care for one another
   (d) bear one another's burdens
   (e) be humble, gentle, patient, bearing with one another in love
   (f) be subject to one another
   (g) don't lie
   (h) forgive; teach and admonish
   (i) encourage one another
   (j) don't speak against one another
   (k) confess your sins to one another and pray for each other
   (l) be humble and submissive
5. Love is patient, kind; does not envy, boast; is not proud, rude, self-seeking, easily angered; keeps no record of wrongs; does not delight in evil; rejoices with the truth; always protects, trusts, hopes, perseveres; never fails.

Chapter 6

1. (a) sexual immorality, impurity and debauchery, idolatry and witchcraft; hatred, discord,

jealousy, fits of rage, selfish ambition, dissensions, factions and envy; drunkenness, orgies; passionate lust, wronging a brother; not knowing God and obeying the gospel of the Lord Jesus; evil desires and greed, anger, malice, slander, filthy language, lies

(b) will not inherit the kingdom of God; punished with everlasting destruction and shut out from the presence of the Lord and from the majesty of his power; the wrath of God

2. (a) separate
   (b) ambassadors

3. think about and put into practice Christ's teachings—things that are true, beautiful, and worthy—and we'll have the peace of God

4. (a) Jesus will bring them with him in resurrection. They will rise first.
   (b) They will be caught up with the believers who had died to meet Jesus in the air. All will be with the Lord forever.

5. (a) The world will not realize or believe what is going to happen
   (b) Keep watch. Be ready and alert because we don't know when it will be.

6. be self-controlled; put on faith, love, and hope; encourage one another and build each other up

7. (a) keep on loving each other
   (b) entertain strangers
   (c) remember those in prison
   (d) honor marriage
   (e) don't love money; be content
   (f) imitate the faith of your leaders
   (g) don't be carried away by strange teachings
   (h) offer God a sacrifice of praise
   (i) do good and share with others
   (j) obey your leaders
   (k) pray

I (name) _____ , completed this book on (date) _____ .

My friend, (name) _____ , or small group, helped me continue my Christian growth by working through my questions with me, and supporting me with kindness and prayer.